USA Basketball

Joe Layden

SCHOLASTIC INC.
New York Toronto London Auckland Sydney

Photo Credits: Book

Cover, 6, 80: NBA Photo Library. **VI, 3, 5, 7, 14, 20, 26, 38, 50, 62, 76:** NBA/Andrew D. Bernstein. **8, 32, 44, 56:** NBA/Nathaniel S. Butler. **68:** NBA/ Scott Cunningham. **71:** NBA/Lou Capozzola. **74, 75:** NBA/Steven Freeman.

Photo Credits: Insert Section

I: NBA Photo Library. **II, V, VII:** NBA/Barry Gossage. **III, VI:** NBA/Nathaniel S. Butler. **IV:** NBA/Norm Perdue. **VIII, XIII (Azzi), XV (Swoopes):** NBA/Scott Cunningham. **IX:** NBA/Andy Hayt. **X:** NBA/Andrew D. Bernstein. **XI:** NBA/Bill Baptist. **XII, XVI (McClain):** NBA/Steven Freeman. **XIII (McGhee), XIV (Lobo/Steding), XV (Leslie/Edwards), XVI (Bolton):** NBA/Lou Capozzola. **XIII (Staley), XVI (McCray):** NBA/Noren Trotman.

ISBN 0-590-89660-1
Copyright © 1996 NBA Properties, Inc.
Copyright © 1996 USA Basketball, Inc.
All rights reserved. Published by Scholastic Inc.

12 11 10 9 8 7 6 5 4 3 2 1   6 7 8 9/9 0 1/0

Printed in the U.S.A.
First Scholastic Printing, May 1996

To Tim — friend, brother, backyard rival.
Writers can't jump, but they sure can dream.

Table of Contents

Michael Jordan flies high.

The 1996 U.S. Olympic Dream Team

Basketball in the 1990's is a global sport. National Basketball Association games can be seen on television throughout the world. Children in Europe and Asia wear jerseys bearing the names and numbers of their favorite NBA stars. It is a simple game whose popularity seems to know no geographic boundaries.

Still, basketball remains a distinct part of the American sporting life. It is part of our culture. That's why we were so proud of our Olympic achievements. Basketball became an Olympic event in 1936, and for 36 years, the U.S. was undefeated, winning 63 consecutive games and seven gold medals.

In the 1972 Olympic Games in Munich, West Germany, the team settled for the silver medal after a controversial loss to the former Soviet Union. And again in 1988, the U.S. lost to the Soviet team and won a bronze medal.

Each loss was difficult to accept, but not just because it was a loss. While other countries sent their best professional players to play in the Olympic Games, NBA players were not allowed to compete until the International Basketball Federation changed its rules in 1989. The Olympic Games became truly open competition with no restrictions on NBA players.

Thus, the "Dream Team" was born. USA Basketball, which selects the U.S. Olympic Basketball team, had the opportunity to invite NBA players, and it assembled the greatest basketball team in history.

The original Dream Team featured NBA legends: Michael Jordan, Larry Bird, Magic Johnson. At first there was concern that some players might not want to participate. After all, there was a chance they might get injured. Instead, every player who received an invitation decided to compete. They were thrilled to have the opportunity to bring a gold medal back to the United States.

That's precisely what they did, too. The Dream Team finished first at the 1992 Olympic Games in Barcelona, Spain, and set a new standard for international basketball. Two years later a second edition of the Dream Team won a gold medal at the World Championship of Basketball in Toronto, Canada.

Now it's time for the 1996 version of the Dream Team, which will represent the United States this summer at the Olympic Games in Atlanta, Georgia. Once again, a remarkably talented group of athletes has been brought together for the express purpose of winning a gold medal in basketball. This Dream Team is an impressive mix of youth and experience. It includes original Dream Team alumni John Stockton, Karl Malone, Scottie Pippen, and David Robinson, as well as veteran NBA stars Hakeem Olajuwon and Reggie Miller. It also features such bright new stars as Shaquille O'Neal, Grant Hill, Anfernee "Penny" Hardaway, and Glenn Robinson. Two more players will be added to the roster before the Games begin.

Like their predecessors, these athletes have chosen to make the sacrifices necessary for Olympic success. There will be no vacations this summer — only work. They will practice together every day. They will get to know one another's strengths and weakness-

Larry Bird battles for position under the boards.

es. Under the guidance of head coach Lenny Wilkens, they will try to become a *team*, rather than a collection of individual superstars. For many of them, the Olympic experience will be the highlight of their careers.

"I think it ranks number one," says Hardaway. "It's not like any other game of basketball. It's for your country. You'll only have a group of guys like this together one time, so you have to cherish the moment."

For the fan, there should be plenty of moments worth cherishing. Imagine Shaq pulling down a rebound and triggering a fast break with Penny Hardaway streaking down the middle, Karl Malone on one wing, and Grant Hill on the other.

Now that's entertainment!

A dream come true—Magic Johnson accepts a gold medal at the 1992 Summer Olympic Games.

1996 U.S. Olympic Dream Team Roster

No.	Name	Pos.	Ht.	Wt.	Birth Date	NBA Team
6	Anfernee Hardaway	Guard	6'7"	200	7/18/72	Orlando Magic
5	Grant Hill	Forward	6'8"	225	10/5/72	Detroit Pistons
11	Karl Malone	Forward	6'9"	256	7/24/63	Utah Jazz
10	Reggie Miller	Guard	6'7"	190	8/24/65	Indiana Pacers
15	Hakeem Olajuwon	Center	7'0"	250	1/21/63	Houston Rockets
13	Shaquille O'Neal	Center	7'1"	301	3/6/72	Orlando Magic
8	Scottie Pippen	Forward	6'7"	225	9/25/65	Chicago Bulls
7	David Robinson	Center	7'1"	235	8/6/65	San Antonio Spurs
14	Glenn Robinson	Forward	6'7"	220	1/10/73	Milwaukee Bucks
12	John Stockton	Guard	6'1"	175	3/26/62	Utah Jazz

Head Coach: Lenny Wilkens, Atlanta Hawks
Assistant Coaches: Bobby Cremins, Georgia Tech; Clem Haskins, University of Minnesota; Jerry Sloan, Utah Jazz

The Coach

The man who leads the Dream Team into Atlanta for the 1996 Olympic Games must be much more than a cheerleader. He must be a talented manager and motivator. He'll have to know how to handle pressure from fans and the media as well as pressure from opposing defenses. He'll be expected to make the proper substitutions. And he'll have to be a diplomat. With this many great athletes on one team, there won't be enough playing time to go around. It is the coach's responsibility to make sure that the players understand and accept their roles, no matter how small.

That's quite a task. Fortunately, in head coach Lenny Wilkens, the Dream Team has the perfect man for the job. A member of the Basketball Hall of Fame, Wilkens was named NBA Coach of the Year in 1994, when he led the Atlanta Hawks to the Eastern Conference Semifinals. In 1979 he guided the Seattle SuperSonics to an NBA championship. He has won more games than any other coach in NBA history. Most important of all, though, Wilkens knows what it's like to be an Olympic coach. He assisted Chuck Daly with the first Dream Team during the 1992 Olympic Games.

One thing is certain. With Lenny Wilkens in charge, the players will listen. "He's the winningest coach, and everybody wants to be coached by the best," says forward Glenn Robinson of the Milwaukee Bucks. "Hopefully, I can learn something. I'll be at full attention at all times."

ANFERNEE HARDAWAY

"Playing in the Olympic Games is like playing in the All-Star Game, but with more firepower."

When the Orlando Magic won the NBA draft lottery for the second consecutive year in 1993, they did what most people expected them to do. They drafted Michigan forward Chris Webber with the number one pick. Within minutes, though, the Magic did the unexpected. They traded Webber to the Golden State Warriors for three future first-round draft picks and a 6' 7" point guard by the name of Anfernee "Penny" Hardaway.

Some people in Orlando were not exactly thrilled with that decision. Webber, after all, had been a star at the University of Michigan, and had played in two consecutive NCAA championship games. Hardaway, the number three pick in the draft, had gotten comparatively little publicity during his career at Memphis State. Sure, he was a pretty slick ballhandler and passes, but was he really *that* good? Magic fans weren't so sure.

"Webber was the safe pick, the logical pick," Orlando General Manager Pat Williams says. "So Penny walked into this hailstorm of controversy."

The storm has long since passed. Penny Hardaway, in just his third professional season, is one of the most popular players in Orlando and one of the brightest young stars in the NBA. His no-look passes and extraordinary court sense remind some observers of another Dream Team point guard: Magic Johnson. The idea of being compared to Magic makes Penny somewhat uncomfortable. He is a shy, humble young man who is embarrassed by the mountain of praise he has received in his brief NBA career. But he clearly deserves the attention.

"Penny is an unbelievable athlete who has great confidence," says San Antonio Spurs center David Robinson, a three-time Olympian. "The things he's been able to accomplish in the league are phenomenal. Here's a guy who is so exciting. He's dunking over guys and running up and down the floor and shooting the three. I played with him one summer before he came into the league and I could tell he was going to be real special then."

Growing Up Tough

Life as a kid in Memphis, Tennessee, wasn't easy for Anfernee Deon Hardaway. He was born July 18, 1972, and grew up in a rough neighborhood, surrounded by drugs and crime and violence. A lot of his friends joined gangs and got into trouble. Some were killed. For Penny, though, making the wrong choice was never really an option. Not with Louise Hardaway nearby.

Louise was Penny's grandmother. She was the one who looked at Anfernee when he was a baby and said, "He's pretty as a penny." Soon, she was calling him simply "Penny," and the kids on the block chimed in. When Penny was 11 years old his mother, Fae Patterson, moved to Los Angeles to pursue a career in the entertainment industry. She wanted to take her son with her, but Louise intervened. "You're not hauling my baby all over the country," she told Fae. From that time on, Penny lived with his grandmother.

By the time he was a senior in high school, Penny was high on the recruiting list of nearly every major college basketball program in the country. He chose to attend school in his hometown, at Memphis State. Penny was already a local legend, and that decision made him even more popular. "The people here just about worship him," says Memphis State coach Larry Finch. "He could have gone to college anywhere, but he stayed right here."

The transition to college was not as smooth as Penny would have liked. He had to sit out his freshman year because he was academically ineligible. Eventually, he would prove to be an exceptional student — he even made the dean's list! But as a freshman, living without basketball for the first time in his life, he became bored and frustrated. Trouble caught up with him one night when he was standing in a neighbor's driveway with a friend. The two young men were robbed at gunpoint. One of the gunmen fired a shot as he was driving away. The bullet bounced off the street and entered Penny's foot, breaking three bones.

Fortunately those wounds healed, and for the next two years Penny dominated the Great Midwestern Conference. As a junior he averaged 22.8 points, 8.5 rebounds, and 6.4 assists per game. He was conference player of the year and first-team All-America. When the season was over, he decided to enter the NBA draft.

The Magic, however, were not sure that Penny was a wise investment. After watching him perform badly at a private workout in Orlando, team officials decided they'd be better off with Chris Webber. Thanks to some words of support from Magic center Shaquille O'Neal, though, Penny was given another chance. Shaq and Penny had met a few months earlier on the set of *Blue Chips,* a film about college basketball. Shaq was impressed by the way Penny played in pickup games and hoped the two could be teammates in Orlando. After a second workout, in which Penny played flawlessly, it was obvious that Shaq would get his wish.

11

For a while, Penny was not very happy in Orlando. The fans booed when his name was announced on draft day. They booed when he appeared in his first exhibition game. And they booed when he replaced Scott Skiles as the starting point guard. Penny handled the pain of that reception with quiet dignity, even though he was deeply hurt by the experience. He continued to work as hard as he could every day in practice. And he hoped that one day the fans in Orlando would accept him as one of their own.

That day wasn't long in coming. Penny averaged 16 points, 5.4 rebounds, and 6.6 assists in his first season. He was runner-up in Rookie of the Year voting. The following year he averaged 20.9 points and 7.2 assists as the Magic reached the NBA Finals for the first time in franchise history. Along the way, Penny was chosen to start at point guard in the 1995 NBA All-Star Game and was named All-NBA First Team. The jeers turned to cheers.

As a member of the Dream Team, Penny is sure to become even more popular. But that isn't what motivates him now. Like his teammates, he wants to win a gold medal. "I can't imagine putting it around my neck, but if that day comes, I'm sure I'll be the proudest basketball player in the world, because it says you have done something for your country," Penny says. "By winning the gold medal, you've done the ultimate."

Just the facts…
About Anfernee Hardaway

Career Statistics

GP	FG%	FT%	Rebounds	Assists	Points	Avg.
159	.490	.758	775	1,095	2,926	18.4

Career Highlights

- National High School Player of the Year (1990)
- First-Team NCAA All-America (1992–93)
- Named to NBA All-Rookie First Team (1993–94)
- Starting point guard in 1995 NBA All-Star Game

Did you know?

Although Penny Hardaway is now considered one of the best point guards in the NBA, he played shooting guard for the first half of his rookie season.

GRANT HILL

"Those who have the opportunity to compete in the Olympic Games are in a select group. To me, it's a wonderful honor."

Wendell Byrd was shocked. The basketball coach at South Lakes High School in Reston, Virginia, had just invited a gangly 14-year-old named Grant Hill to try out for the varsity team. He expected the kid to be happy. Instead, Grant broke down and cried.

"I just didn't want to jump over my friends," he says now. "I wanted to be liked. I didn't want to seem better than everybody else."

A lot has changed since Grant was a shy, awkward teenager. Today, as one of the best basketball players in the world, he is a young man comfortable with his talent and the stardom that comes with it. In fact, Grant, a 6' 8" forward for the Detroit Pistons, is one of the most popular players in the game. He shared NBA Rookie of the Year honors with Jason Kidd of the Dallas Mavericks in 1995. But Grant has received nearly as much praise for his conduct off the court.

Grant was taught the formula for success at a young age. His father, Calvin Hill, attended Yale University and went on to become an All-Pro running back with the Dallas Cowboys and Washington Redskins. His mother, Janet, is an attorney who graduated from Wellesley College. Watching his parents, Grant learned a valuable lesson: There is no substitute for hard work.

Unfortunately, as much as Grant loved and admired his parents, he also had a difficult time growing up in their shadows. From the day he was born, on October 5, 1972, expectations for Grant Henry Hill were extremely high. He was encouraged to develop both his mind and his body. So he played soccer and basketball — but not until his homework was done. He also took piano lessons.

As the only child of two highly successful parents, Grant had more opportunities than many of his friends. He lived in a big house and traveled all over the world. He met a lot of famous people. But there were difficulties, too. For one thing, Grant was concerned that some of his friends liked him only because his father had been a famous athlete. He worried constantly about disappointing people — especially his parents.

The pressure of growing up in the spotlight made Grant want to withdraw. He just wanted to be a normal kid; part of the group. Eventually, though, Grant realized that there was nothing wrong with fulfilling his potential. If he was good enough to play on the varsity basketball team as a freshman, then that was where he belonged. His friends would have to understand.

As it turned out, they did. In fact, they admired him. Grant went on to have an exceptional high school career. He led South Lakes to the semifinals of the state high school basketball tournament twice, and was named Northern Virginia Player of the Year three times. As a senior, he averaged 30 points per game and became one of the most highly recruited players in the nation.

Big Man on Campus

Grant could have selected any college in the country, but he decided to attend Duke University, in Durham, North Carolina. Grant liked Duke because it not only had a great basketball team, but also was a fine academic institution. And he was impressed by coach Mike Krzyzewski, who was considered one of the most intelligent and honorable men in college basketball. Of course, Krzyzewski was equally impressed with Grant.

"Grant Hill is the best player I ever coached," Krzyzewski would later say. "But he's a reluctant superstar. To his credit, he doesn't want to separate himself from the team."

Grant played on some great college basketball teams at Duke. The Blue Devils won national championships in his freshman and sophomore seasons. Grant was content to blend into the background on those teams, which featured such future NBA players as Bobby Hurley and Christian Laettner. But there were times when his sheer talent and athleticism commanded attention. In the semifinal of the 1991 NCAA tournament at the Hoosier Dome in Indianapolis, for example, Grant was asked to guard future NBA player Stacey Augmon of the University of Nevada-Las Vegas. UNLV was the defending champion, and Augmon was one of its best players. But with Grant covering him tightly, Augmon scored only six points that night and Duke won the game. Two nights later, in the first minute of the NCAA title game against Kansas, Grant mesmerized the crowd by soaring high above the basket to take a lob pass and throwing down a spectacular dunk. He was only a freshman, but clearly he was destined for stardom.

By the time he was a senior at Duke, Grant was prepared to accept the fact that he couldn't afford to merely blend in. The Blue Devils needed more than that. He was one of the most talented players in college basketball, and it was time to start demonstrating what he could do. It was time to take the advice of coach Krzyzewski, who told Grant, "Don't be afraid to be good."

Grant's senior year was exceptional. He led Duke in scoring (17.4 points per game), assists, and steals, and was named first-team All-America. To his delight, he also discovered that by taking a more aggressive role, he helped the team flourish. The Blue Devils went to the championship game of the 1994 NCAA Tournament before losing to the University of Arkansas 76–72.

On 1994 NBA Draft Day, Grant was selected by the Detroit Pistons, who had the third pick. Detroit's director of player personnel, Billy McKinney, was so happy to have drafted Grant that he broke into tears. "We've talked a lot about the kinds of people we want to acquire to help us get back to the top," McKinney said at the time. I had a little formula — TCTP — Talent, Character, and a Team Player. Grant Hill embodies that phrase. He's the consummate professional."

Since going to Detroit, Grant has done nothing to discourage predictions of greatness. He led the team in scoring as a rookie with an average of 19.9 points per game, and was a starter in the 1995 NBA All-Star Game. A smooth and versatile player, he can handle any position on the floor. His quickness, leaping ability, and deft outside shot continue to invite comparisons to the greatest player the game has ever known: Michael Jordan.

Grant modestly shrugs off such comparisons. For now he is content to find his own place in the basketball world. He is honored to have been selected for the Dream Team.

"This is by far the highlight of my career," Grant says. "I can't think of anything in my career, in my life, that excites me like this. Every time I think to myself that I'm on the Olympic team, I feel like a little kid."

Just the facts...
About Grant Hill

Career Statistics

GP	FG%	FT%	Rebounds	Assists	Points	Avg.
70	.477	.732	445	353	1,394	19.9

Career Highlights

- Won two NCAA titles at Duke University (1991, 1992)
- Co-NBA Rookie of the Year in 1995
- Named a starter in 1995 NBA All-Star Game
- Led Detroit Pistons in scoring in 1994–95

Did you know?

In 1995, Grant Hill became the only rookie ever to receive the most fan votes in balloting for the NBA All-Star Game.

KARL MALONE

*"To be on the Olympic team really says
something. I think my kids and I will enjoy
it one day when we watch the videotape.
I want to tell my son and daughter,
'Yeah, that's your dad right there.'"*

n the summer of 1984, Karl Malone had just finished his sopho-more year at Louisiana Tech University. He was invited to try out for the United States Olympic basketball team, which at that time was comprised entirely of amateur players. The experience meant the world to Karl, a shy country kid from Summerfield, Louisiana. He worked as hard as he could at the U.S. Olympic Team Trials, and felt he had earned a place on the team. In the end, though, he was not one of the twelve players selected by coach Bob Knight.

Today, Karl is an NBA superstar. The 6'9", 256-pound power forward with the Utah Jazz has proven himself countless times over the course of his 12-year professional career. He is the team's all-time leading scorer and rebounder. He's also a nine-time NBA All-Star and seven-time All-NBA First-Team selection.

Despite those accomplishments, though, Karl occasionally thinks back to 1984. Not making the U.S. Olympic Team was one of the greatest disappointments of his life. That's why he feels so privileged to be a member of the 1996 Dream Team. "I was one of the last players cut from the team in 1984," Karl says. "It was kind of a slap in the face, saying, in essence, 'You're not good enough to play on the Olympic team.' But I can look back and say, 'OK, now I've played on two teams.'"

Indeed he can. Karl is one of only four basketball players selected to represent the United States in both 1992 and 1996. He was the third-leading scorer and second-leading rebounder on the original Dream Team, which captured the gold medal at the Olympic Games in Barcelona, Spain, in 1992. Karl has shown no signs of slowing down since then, so it was hardly a surprise that he was invited back.

Karl overcame long odds to make it to the NBA. His mother, Shirley, raised nine children on her own. Karl spent most of his spare time fishing and playing basketball. He started out practicing on a homemade hoop in his backyard. "We did everything the old-fashioned way," Karl says. "We'd get an old bicycle tire, knock the spokes out of it and put haywire on it. That was our basket."

Karl was a standout at Summerfield High, but he had his problems at Louisiana Tech. He was extremely upset when he arrived at the school and discovered that he was academically ineligible to play basketball. He would have to sit out a year and concentrate exclusively on his classwork. But worse than the frustration of not being able to play basketball was the embarrassment he felt. "I had let my family down," Karl remembers. "I had let Karl Malone down. I was at the point where I said, 'Karl, are you going to be a loser the rest of your life, or are you going to do something positive with yourself?'"

Over the years, he's answered that question quite clearly. Karl is not a loser. Through hard work and dedication, he became a good student and world-class basketball player. In three seasons at Louisiana Tech he averaged 18.7 points and 9.3 rebounds. It was there that he earned the nickname "The Mailman" because of his ability to deliver in clutch situations. By the end of his junior year, he knew it was time to find a job in the NBA.

Impact Player

Utah, which had the thirteenth pick in the first round, was the team fortunate enough to get Karl. From the moment he arrived in the league, his presence was felt. He averaged 14.9 points and 8.9 rebounds in his first season, and was named to the 1985–86 NBA All-Rookie Team. But that was merely a glimpse of things to come. In his second year Karl became an offensive force, averaging 21.7 points and 10.4 rebounds. Since then he has averaged at least 25 points per game in each season. In 1989–90, Karl had perhaps his finest season. He averaged 31 points and 11.1 rebounds.

By that time, Karl had developed a close relationship with Jazz point guard John Stockton. The two had not only become good friends, but also had come to thoroughly understand each other's strengths and weaknesses. Today it is hard to think of one without thinking of the other. Karl is the Jazz career scoring leader primarily because Stockton has passed the ball to him in the open court on thousands of occasions. And Stockton is the NBA's career leader in assists primarily because he has Karl Malone on his team. What really separates Karl from other power forwards is his work ethic. Early in his NBA career, Karl decided that he was going to refine his natural ability. He looked at his body as if it were a lump of clay. And he began to sculpt it. After practice sessions he would retreat to the weight room and pump iron for hours. He lifted until his body ached. And then he lifted some more. Gradually, he began to notice a difference. He lost some of his baby fat. He felt better. And he looked better.

Now Karl has the sculpted physique of a bodybuilder and the strength of a tight end. Once he gets position under the basket, there is almost no one who can take a rebound away from him. "I don't think there's ever been anybody chiseled like Karl Malone, who can do what he does," says Miami Heat coach Pat Riley. "Every play, every rebound, you are going to have to go harder than you would go against anybody else in the league."

There are a few holes on Karl's resume. He has never won an NBA title, for example, and at 33 years of age, time is running out. Even if he never acquires a championship ring, though, Karl has had quite a run in the world of professional basketball. He considers the first Dream Team experiences to be among the highlights of his career.

Karl's familiarity with international competition and Olympic pressure will be of great value to the Dream Team in Atlanta. "I think there's some leadership role there," he says. "I think I'll expect out of my teammates what they expect out of me: Go out and play hard and carry yourself on and off the court the way you're supposed to. You are representing your country."

Just the facts...
About Karl Malone

Career Statistics

GP	FG%	FT%	Rebounds	Assists	Points	Avg.
816	.526	.721	8,929	2,470	21,237	26.0

Career Highlights

- Nine-time NBA All-Star
- MVP of NBA All-Star Game (1989, 1993)
- Won Olympic Gold Medal in 1992
- Utah Jazz' all-time leader in points and rebounds

Did you know?

Karl Malone loves Country and Western music. One of his favorite performers is Garth Brooks.

REGGIE MILLER

"When they let the professionals start playing in the Olympic Games, I was wondering if it was going to pass me by or if I was good enough to make it. This is fantastic!"

When the Dream Team needs someone to loosen up an opposing defense by knocking down a few long-range bombs, it will surely turn to Reggie Miller. The 6' 7", 190-pound guard for the Indiana Pacers is one of the best outside shooters in NBA history. For him, there is no shot too long, no coverage that can't be broken. And when the pressure is on, Reggie really rises to the occasion. You can see it on his face. When the game gets tight and the clock winds down, Reggie starts to smile. He wants the ball in his hands.

"Like most great players," says Pacers president Donnie Walsh, "Reggie seems to get better as the stakes get higher."

Though he grew up in a loving, stable household that placed a premium on athletics, Reggie did not seem destined for greatness. Far from it, actually. The youngest son of Carrie and Saul Miller was born on August 24, 1965, in Riverside, California. He was a delicate child whose hips were so badly twisted that he was forced to sleep with steel braces on his legs until he was four years old. He wore corrective shoes on his feet. Doctors told Carrie and Saul that their son would probably never be able to walk normally, let alone play sports.

The Millers thanked the doctors for their help, but decided to ignore the prognosis. They gave Reggie all the support he needed. When he'd sit in the house and stare out the window while his brothers and sisters played basketball in the driveway, they would comfort and reassure him. One day, they said, he'd be able to join them.

"My parents kept me positive," Reggie says. "They were persistent in making sure I did the same things as the other kids. They weren't going to let it affect the rest of my life."

In a way, however, the experience did affect Reggie's entire life. It not only made him more determined than ever to succeed as an athlete, it also made him more sensitive to those less fortunate. Today Reggie devotes considerable time and resources to such organizations as the United Negro College Fund. He also runs a basketball camp for kids and is a frequent visitor to hospital pediatric wards.

When he was old enough and healthy enough to take part in the family games, Reggie found the competition to be a bit rougher than he expected. It was bad enough that older brothers, Saul, Jr., and Darrell, routinely slapped the ball back in his face. But when Reggie's sister started rejecting his shots, that really made him angry.

Of course, Reggie's big sister wasn't just any player. Cheryl Miller, who is two years older than Reggie, went on to become a star at the University of Southern California. In 1995 she was inducted into the Basketball Hall of Fame. Reggie spent much of his early career toiling in Cheryl's long and imposing shadow. No matter what he did, it was never quite as impressive as Cheryl's accomplishments. There was, for example, the night he scored 39 points in a high school game. Reggie was so excited he couldn't wait to get home and brag to his big sister. Cheryl also had a game that night, though, and when Reggie walked in the door he discovered that she, too, had played pretty well. In fact, she had scored *105* points!

A Talented Family

The Millers were an ambitious bunch. Saul, Jr., like his dad, went into the military. He played saxophone in the Air Force band. Darrell was a catcher with the California Angels for five years; he now works in the team's front office. Cheryl, in addition to her exploits as a player, has been a coach at USC and a television broadcaster. And Tammy, the baby of the family, is a lawyer. With all of that competition, Reggie had no choice but to succeed.

Of course, having Cheryl as a sister did have its advantages. When they were teenagers, sometimes Reggie and Cheryl would visit playgrounds around Los Angeles and hustle games of two-on-two against unsuspecting opponents. They rarely lost.

By the time he entered the University of California at Los Angeles (UCLA), Reggie was a tough and talented basketball player. His long high jump shot, along with a fierce desire to win, had been refined in backyard games against taller opponents. He was remarkably skinny, but not nearly as frail as he appeared. As a matter of fact, Reggie took great pride in his ability to handle emotional and physical stress. If an opponent knocked him down, he bounced back up. When fans on the road tried to annoy him by chanting "*Cheryl! Cheryl!*" he simply played harder.

Reggie's finest moment as a pro came against the Knicks in Game 5 of the 1994 Eastern Conference Finals. In front of a raucous crowd at Madison Square Garden, he scored 25 points *in the fourth quarter* to lead the Pacers to a come-from-behind 93−86 victory. Reggie's performance that night was incredible. With Knick defenders chasing him all over the floor, and the fans booing every time he touched the ball, he hit an NBA-record five three-point field goals in the last 12 minutes. The Pacers lost that series in seven games, but when it was over, everyone knew that Reggie Miller was one of the best players in the NBA. Finally, he had stepped out of the shadows.

In 1995 Reggie again led the Pacers to the Eastern Conference Finals. He also played in his second NBA All-Star Game. When the season was over, he was an obvious choice to represent the United States in Olympic competition.

"I'm very excited," Reggie says. "I think just because I played in the World Championship, being selected to the Olympic team wasn't to be taken for granted. Toronto was exciting, but being in the Olympic Games for your country is fantastic."

Just the facts...
About Reggie Miller

Career Statistics

GP	FG%	FT%	Rebounds	Assists	Points	Avg.
644	.493	.879	2,056	2,067	12,467	19.4

Career Highlights

- Three-time NBA All-Star (1990, 1995, 1996)
- Indiana Pacers' all-time scoring leader
- Selected for Dream Team in 1994 and 1996
- Led NBA in free throw percentage (.918) in 1994–95

Did you know?

Reggie Miller is the third-leading scorer in UCLA history, behind Don MacLean and Kareem Abdul-Jabbar (formerly known as Lew Alcindor).

HAKEEM OLAJUWON

"Winning a gold medal in the Olympic Games is the biggest accomplishment for any individual. It seemed so far off, so unreachable. But if you take it step by step, you are there before you know it."

They call Hakeem Olajuwon "The Dream." But for the longest time he thought his own personal dream would go unfulfilled. Hakeem, the 7'0", 250-pound center for the Houston Rockets, is one of the greatest players in NBA history. He has a pair of championship rings. What he really wants, though, is a chance to represent the United States in Olympic competition.

It became a goal of Hakeem's in 1992, when professionals were invited to compete in basketball for the first time. Hakeem watched the original Dream Team overwhelm the competition in Barcelona, Spain. He watched his friends win a gold medal. And as he watched, he wanted to be with them. He was talented enough, of course. As loaded as the Dream Team was, it still could have used Hakeem's services. However, he was not a United States citizen. Hakeem was born in Lagos, Nigeria, on January 21, 1963, and did not come to the United States until he was a college freshman. He became a United States citizen in 1993, but still had to petition the International Basketball Federation (FIBA) for special permission to represent his adopted country. When he received that permission, Hakeem became a lock to make the latest version of the Dream Team, which will compete in the 1996 Olympic Games in Atlanta.

"In the beginning, because of the rules, it looked like I would be unable to play," Hakeem says. "So that dream was lost for a while. This was just another example of having faith, not losing hope. This is a great opportunity for me, to play for the United States when I thought it was impossible."

The story of Hakeem Abdul Olajuwon is the stuff of legend. He was raised in a country where almost no one knew anything about basketball. Much of Nigeria is poor, but Hakeem was fortunate to have grown up in a middle-class family. His parents owned a cement company. They initially discouraged Hakeem, the third of their six children, from participating in sports. But one of Hakeem's older brothers was able to convince their parents that Hakeem had some athletic ability and that he should be encouraged to develop that talent.

Initially, basketball wasn't high on his list of favorite sports. Hakeem liked to play soccer and team handball, both of which are very popular in Nigeria. It was while he was playing team handball at a national sports festival that 15-year-old Hakeem was introduced to basketball. An American Peace Corps worker named Oliver Johnson took one look at Hakeem's size and strength and thought the kid should give basketball a try.

"I played once," Hakeem says, "and I fell in love with the game."

Coming to America

After graduating from high school in Lagos, Hakeem accepted a basketball scholarship to the University of Houston. When he arrived on campus he was a shy, awkward young man who was overwhelmed by the differences in culture and language. In time, though, he began to adjust. He spent a full year concentrating on his classwork. Then he began developing his body. In Nigeria, Hakeem had always relied on natural ability. He never bothered to get in shape. At Houston he had to prepare his body for the stress that it would face in games.

Hakeem developed quickly. In fact, by the spring of 1984, he was ready for the NBA. He had led the Cougars to the NCAA championship game in 1983 and 1984, and had been named to several All-America teams. Most NBA scouts expected Hakeem to be a high first-round draft pick. As it turned out, he was the very first pick. And since that pick belonged to the Houston Rockets, Hakeem didn't even have to leave town!

Over the past 12 years Hakeem has been one of the most consistent and productive players in the NBA. He has played in ten All-Star Games. He has been named to the NBA All-Defensive First Team seven times and was Defensive Player of the Year in 1993 and 1994. He was also Most Valuable Player in 1994.

Some of Hakeem's best games have come in the playoffs, which is why he is considered a great clutch performer. He led the Rockets to the NBA Championship in 1994 and 1995. Both years he was named MVP of the NBA Finals.

"Hakeem is finally getting the respect he deserves," says Utah Jazz forward Karl Malone. "A lot of things enter into winning a championship, but without a doubt I think he's carried that team both years."

Hakeem would probably dispute that claim, since he is the ultimate team player. When he was presented with the MVP trophy, he insisted that his Houston teammates join him in the celebration. "You don't know how good that made us feel," says Houston Rockets guard Mario Elie. "That's the thing about Hakeem. He knows that it takes the entire team to win."

A devout Muslim, Hakeem is a humble, quiet man. Until 1991, he was commonly known as "Akeem" because the "H" in his name is silent. Finally, though, Hakeem corrected the mistake. Now, of course, everyone knows his name — and his reputation. Hakeem can beat his man with strength and power inside, or he can hit a fadeaway jumper. His trademark "Dreamshake" move involves three or four head fakes, followed by a layup or dunk. He's also a spectacular defender.

For Hakeem, the entire Olympic experience is going to be a pleasure — even the workouts. "I think the practices will be more competitive than the games," he says. "In the games, we will become a team."

A team that Hakeem fully expects to finish first. But he is taking nothing for granted. "This is the opportunity of a lifetime and you have to take advantage of it," he says. "It's not tough to be motivated to be in the Olympic Games."

Not at all. And if they drape the gold medal around his neck, Hakeem's dream will have come true.

Just the facts...
About Hakeem Olajuwon

Career Statistics

GP	FG%	FT%	Rebounds	Assists	Points	Avg.
828	.516	.710	10,239	2,135	19,904	24.0

Career Highlights

- Named NBA Most Valuable Player in 1994
- Eleven-time NBA All-Star
- Voted MVP of NBA Finals in 1994 and 1995
- Five-time All-NBA First Team

Did you know?

When Hakeem played at the University of Houston, the Cougars dunked so often and so spectacularly that they were nicknamed "Phi Slama Jama."

SHAQUILLE O'NEAL

*"Winning a gold medal at the World Championship
was fine, but the Olympic Games would be ever better.
It would be really special."*

Sometimes there aren't enough hours in the day for Shaquille O'Neal. In addition to his regular job as center for the Orlando Magic, Shaq moonlights as a rap singer, movie star, commercial spokesman, and businessman. At only 24 years of age, he is one of the busiest and most successful athletes in the world. And this summer, Shaq will be busier and more visible than ever. As the 7' 1", 301-pound man in the middle for the Dream Team, he will be the center of attention at the 1996 Olympic Games.

"Shaq is so big," says fellow Dream Teamer Grant Hill. "He's big and athletic and knows how to play the game. The thing I really love about him is that he works hard and plays hard on both ends of the court."

As confident and talented as Shaq is today, it's hard to imagine that there was a time when he was awkward and unsure of himself. But there was. Shaq was born on March 6, 1972, in Newark, New Jersey. He was not a particularly big baby, just 7 pounds, 11 ounces, but he was a handful right from the start. His mother, Lucille, wanted the boy to have a unique name, so she chose Shaquille Rashaun. In Islamic, Shaquille means "little one," and Rashaun means "warrior."

"I was never very little," Shaq would later write in his autobiography, *Shaq Attack*, "but I was always a warrior."

That attitude would help Shaq later in life, especially on the basketball court. But as a kid, he sometimes went looking for trouble. "People look at me now and think I was an angel," Shaq says. "But I was bad. I wanted people to look at me, so to get attention, I'd get into trouble."

Fortunately, when Shaq messed up, he heard about it. His stepfather, Phillip Harrison, who married Lucille when Shaq was two years old, did not tolerate disobedience. Mr. Harrison was a staff sergeant in the U.S. Army. He was a very serious man who wanted to provide a good life for his children. In return, he insisted that they behave properly. When they got into trouble, he was quick to punish. And Shaq felt his wrath most often. "I always told Shaquille that the world has too many clowns and followers," Mr. Harrison says. "What he needed to be was a leader."

Eventually, Shaq cleaned up his act and tried to meet the standards set by his parents. He discovered that his life began to improve almost immediately. His grades got better in school and he acquired more friends. "I had to find out the hard way," Shaq says. "Thank goodness I had parents who loved me enough to stay on my case."

Shaq's father was transferred often, so the family spent several years living in Europe. It was on a military base in Germany that he first met Dale Brown, the basketball coach at Louisiana State University. Brown, who was conducting a clinic, dragged Shaq out of the audience and asked him to attempt a half-court shot. The ball bounced off the rim. Brown gave the kid a pat on the back and sent him back into the audience. Afterward, Shaq introduced himself to the coach and asked for some conditioning tips. Brown gave him some advice, then looked at the 6' 8", 230-pound athlete in front of him and said, "How long you been in the army, soldier?" When the answer came, Brown nearly fainted. The "soldier" was a 13-year-old boy.

Walking Tall

Shaq matured during his time at Cole High School in San Antonio, Texas. In junior high he had been self-conscious about his size. He would hunch over when he walked, or he'd slide down into his seat, to appear smaller. Kids taunted and insulted him. In high school, though, Shaq became a hero, a star. He walked upright, with his head held high. He smiled a lot. If someone was insensitive enough to make fun of him, he would simply ignore that person. He was trying to become a leader, just as his father had suggested.

Shaq's growth continued in college. He filled out, became stronger. He averaged 21.6 points and 13.5 rebounds per game during his three years at LSU. As a sophomore and junior he was named first-team All-America by *The Sporting News*. Shaq declared himself eligible for the NBA draft in the spring of his junior year. To the surprise of absolutely no one, he was the number one pick of the Orlando Magic. Shortly after the draft, Shaq and his family flew to Orlando. At the airport he charmed a crowd of reporters and fans by saying, "I'm looking forward to going to Disney World and chillin' with Mickey."

It was an appropriate reference, since Shaq has become a pretty popular tourist attraction in his own right. His on-court exploits have become almost legendary. Shaq is so strong, so big, it's almost scary. He can be fierce and intimidating during the game. But off the floor, however, he is a gracious, likeable young man. Fans love him, particularly young fans. And advertisers love him too. The endorsement deals have rolled in. Shaq has become one of the hottest properties in professional sports. "He's got it all," says Magic Johnson, who knows something about charm. "Shaq's got the smile and the talent and the charisma."

There are still some weaknesses in Shaq's game, however. He has to develop a better outside shot and he needs to be more consistent at the free throw line. But he remains one of the most dominant centers in NBA history. In Atlanta, he'll be teaming up with two other 7-footers, Hakeem Olajuwon and David Robinson, to give the United States an awesome inside game.

"It's almost unfair to the other countries for us to have those three guys on our team," says Shaq's Orlando Magic teammate Penny Hardaway. "Any of those guys can score at will."

ANFERNEE HARDAWAY

GRANT HILL

KARL MALONE

REGGIE MILLER

HAKEEM OLAJUWON

SHAQUILLE O'NEAL

SCOTTIE PIPPEN

DAVID ROBINSON

GLENN ROBINSON

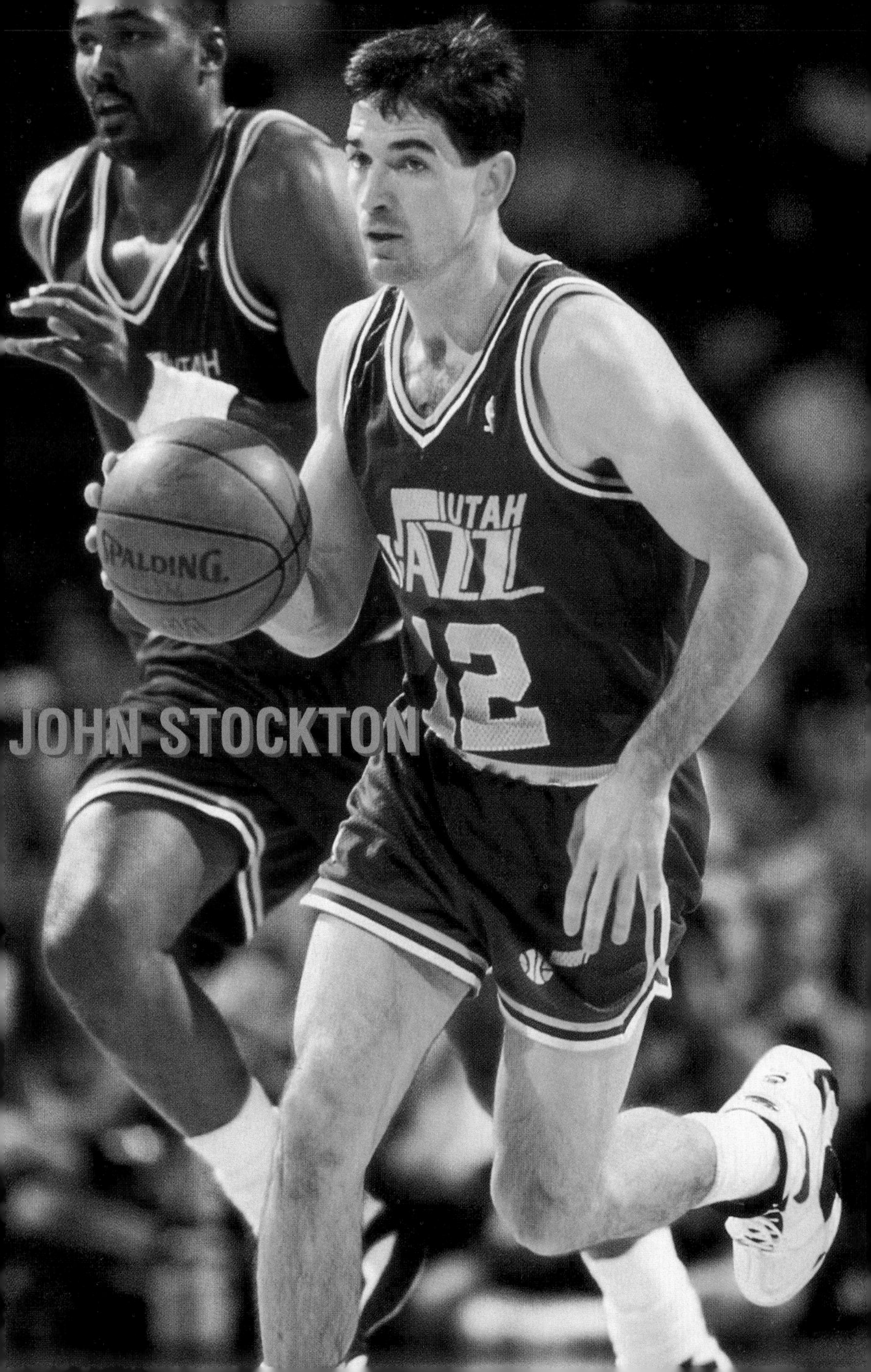

JOHN STOCKTON

USA BASKETBALL WOMEN'S NATIONAL TEAM

CARLA MCGHEE

DAWN STALEY

JENNIFER AZZI

REBECCA LOBO

LISA LESLIE

TERESA EDWARDS

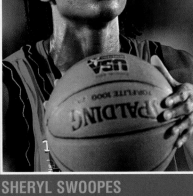

SHERYL SWOOPES

KATRINA MCCLAIN

RUTHIE BOLTON

NIKKI MCCRAY

Just the facts...
About Shaquille O'Neal

Career Statistics

GP	FG%	FT%	Rebounds	Assists	Points	Avg.
241	.583	.558	3,095	561	6,585	27.3

Career Highlights

- Number-one pick in 1992 NBA Draft
- NBA Rookie of the Year in 1993
- MVP 1994 World Championship of Basketball
- Led NBA in scoring (29.3 ppg) in 1994–1995

Did you know?

In 1993 Shaquille O'Neal became the youngest player ever to take part in an NBA All-Star Game.

SCOTTIE PIPPEN

"There is always pressure when you are considered the best and everyone is trying to knock you off. Realistically, we are going to be our only pressure, because we realize that we should be able to beat any team."

When the phone call came from Rod Thorn, the chairman of the USA Basketball Men's Senior National Team Committee, Scottie Pippen was thrilled. Thorn wanted to know if Scottie was interested in being a member of the Dream Team. Scottie couldn't say yes fast enough. For the second time in his career, he'd have a chance to wear the uniform of the United States Olympic men's basketball team.

"It was really exciting," says Scottie, a 6' 7" forward for the Chicago Bulls. "I felt like I had achieved another goal that I wanted to achieve, and that is the opportunity to play on the Olympic team here in the United States."

Scottie was a member of the original Dream Team, which won a gold medal at the 1992 Olympic Games in Barcelona. That, of course, was a very special team. It was the first Olympic Team from the United States to include professional players, and featured such legends as Larry Bird, Magic Johnson, and Michael Jordan. Fast company, to be sure, but Scottie held his own. In fact, he led the team in assists with an average of 5.9 per game.

Scottie has wonderful memories of his first Olympic experience, and he knows it can never be duplicated. But there is also something special about the 1996 Games, because Atlanta, Georgia is the host city. Scottie says, "To be able to come home and feel like it's a homecourt advantage to have your U.S. jersey on is going to stand for a lot."

What Scottie Pippen brings to the Dream Team is a combination of skills unsurpassed in the NBA. He will be one of the team's best outside shooters. He'll also be one of its best ballhandlers, passers, and rebounders. There are no real weaknesses in Scottie's game. He can play point guard, shooting guard, small forward, or power forward.

That diversity helped the Bulls win three consecutive championships, but it wasn't until Michael Jordan's premature and temporary retirement in 1993 that Scottie demonstrated just how valuable a player he was. Most observers predicted a dramatic fall for the Bulls in Jordan's absence, but with Scottie leading the way, they won 55 games — only 2 fewer than the previous year. Scottie had his finest statistical season as a pro. He averaged 22 points, 8.7 rebounds, and 5.6 assists.

Scottie played so well that year that he made a lasting impression on fans across the country. One of his many admirers is Milwaukee Bucks forward Glenn Robinson, a second-year pro who is now one of Pippen's Olympic teammates. "I'm looking forward to playing with Scottie," Robinson says. "Since I grew up in Gary [Indiana], we got a lot of Chicago Bulls games on TV, and he was a guy I watched when I was a kid."

Big Dreams

Hardly anyone predicted greatness for Scottie Maurice Pippen when he was a kid growing up in tiny Hamburg, Arkansas. Born on September 25, 1965, he was the youngest child of Preston and Ethel Pippen. Scottie passed the time by playing basketball. He loved pickup games, but if no one else was around, he'd just shoot and dribble for hours on end. In junior high school he also played football. By high school, though, he concentrated exclusively on basketball. He was determined to be not only the greatest athlete ever to come out of Hamburg, but the first to play in the NBA.

There was just one slight problem. Scottie wasn't very good. A classic late bloomer, he was just a shade over six feet tall as a senior in high school. He was rail thin and not particularly quick, which is why he started only one season at Hamburg High. "He was just an average kid who didn't get into trouble," says his mother. "He never made you think he'd do anything special. But we loved him then and we love him now."

Scottie wanted more than acceptance from his own family. He wanted to play college ball. So he asked his high school coach, Donald Wayne, for help. Wayne put in a call to a friend who coached the basketball team at the University of Central Arkansas and made a pitch on Scottie's behalf. The kid was only 6' 1", Wayne said, but he was still growing. With a little luck, he might develop.

The coach at Central Arkansas, Don Dyer, agreed to let Scottie be a part of the team — as a player/manager. Scottie had no choice but to say yes. He didn't have any other offers. As a freshman he picked up after the other players and practiced every day. On game nights he usually sat on the bench and watched. Over the course of the season, though, there were changes in Scottie. He was 6' 3" by the end of his freshman year. When he returned to campus as a sophomore he was 6' 5" and quite capable of playing with the varsity. He averaged 18.5 points per game that season. By the time he left Central Arkansas he was 6' 7".

Because Central Arkansas received little national exposure,

very few people knew about Scottie Pippen prior to the NBA try-out camps in 1988. But word quickly got around. He was the kid with the long arms, smooth shooting stroke, and expressionless face. That came to be one of Scottie's trademarks: He never showed any emotion on the floor. He just played.

The Seattle SuperSonics made Scottie the fifth pick in the NBA draft. And the Chicago Bulls were so impressed by Scottie that they immediately arranged a trade with Seattle. It was a remarkable turn of events. Four years earlier there wasn't a single Division I basketball program willing to offer him a full scholarship. Now he was in the NBA. "It's just amazing," Scottie says.

As one of only four men on the Dream Team roster who also played in Barcelona, he has the advantage of knowing what to expect from Olympic competition. He knows that the United States, despite its talent, will be challenged on the road to the gold medal.

"We'll face some good players out there," Scottie says. "So we have to understand that there aren't any egos. We have to feel that nobody is being the star of the team. We've got to all jell and let our talents fall into place."

Just the facts...
About Scottie Pippen

Career Statistics

GP	FG%	FT%	Rebounds	Assists	Points	Avg.
630	.489	.688	3,940	3,271	10,994	17.5

Career Highlights

- Member of three consecutive NBA championship teams (1991, 1992, 1993)
- Won Olympic Gold Medal in 1992
- Six-time NBA All-Star
- Named to All-NBA First Team in 1994 and 1995

Did you know?

Scottie Pippen was the youngest child in a very large family. He has 11 older brothers and sisters!

DAVID ROBINSON

"This Dream Team will make its own identity in the Olympic Games. Then, as individuals, we'll have to live up to the label of some of the players we had on the '92 Olympic Team."

More than most professional athletes, David Robinson understands and appreciates the special nature of Olympic competition. The 7'1", 235-pound center for the San Antonio Spurs is the only member of the Dream Team who has played on three U.S. Olympic Teams. In 1988 he helped the United States win a bronze medal at the Olympic Games in Seoul, South Korea. In 1992 he was a key player on the original Dream Team, which easily won a gold medal in Barcelona, Spain. And, now, here he is again.

Representing his country is not a responsibility David takes lightly. After all, this is a man who attended the U.S. Naval Academy and then spent two years serving in the military. The pride he feels is unique. That's why he was more than happy to accept an invitation to play on the Dream Team, even though it meant he'd have to sacrifice a summer at home with his wife and two children.

"This is what I do," David explains. "It's my job. It's how I make my living. To be able to step up and be one of the best is worth far more than that time would be worth having off. I'll miss the time with my kids, because they're at an age where I can have a big impact on them. But this is the opportunity of a lifetime. It's hard to pass up."

When he was a child, it seemed highly unlikely that David would ever play on one Olympic team, let alone three. Not that he wasn't a promising child. He was. It's just that he wasn't all that impressive an athlete.

Born on August 6, 1965, in Key West, Florida, David Maurice Robinson grew up in a middle-class family. When he was still a baby, the family moved to Virginia Beach, Virginia. David's father, Ambrose, was a sonar operator in the Navy. His mother, Freda, was a nurse. They gave their three children a lot of love and guidance, but they were also strict parents. They expected their kids to be good students and good people.

Grades were not usually a problem for David. He was a bright, inquisitive child who loved science, math, and music. To this day, David uses music as a way to relax. He brings a keyboard on the road and often composes songs in his spare time. There was a running joke around the Robinson household when David was a boy. He was such a smart and versatile child that his parents weren't sure who he wanted to be like when he grew up: Mozart, Thomas Edison, or Mick Jagger.

Late Bloomer

Oddly enough, no one mentioned Bill Russell, the Hall of Fame center for the Boston Celtics, with whom David has often been compared. The reason they never mentioned Russell — or any other basketball player — was because David didn't care for the game all that much. He was only 5' 5" when he entered high school, and not much of a player. Four years later he had grown to 6' 6" and was beginning to show great potential. But the game still did not come naturally to him. David preferred gymnastics to basketball. And he preferred academic work to any sport. David scored quite well on his college entrance exams and received a Presidential appointment to the U.S. Naval Academy.

By the time he entered the Naval Academy, David was 6' 7", only one inch below the maximum height that the Navy allows for its students. Once there, though, they could not dismiss him, even if he continued to grow. And David did keep growing. More than an inch per year. By the time he was a senior, David was 7'1", and suddenly an awful lot of people thought he looked like one of the best college basketball players in the country.

His improvement did not happen by accident. David considered his physical size to be a gift, just as his intelligence was a gift. And he felt obligated to develop that gift to its fullest. So he lifted weights and worked on his dribbling and shooting. He became a student of the game. In time, all of the effort paid off. David led the nation in rebounding as a junior. In 1987, as a senior, he averaged 28.2 points and 11.8 rebounds and was named College Player of the Year.

David was sought by every team in the NBA. But there was a catch. As a Naval Academy graduate, he was obligated to serve at least two years in the military. Of course, a lot could happen in two years. It was possible that David's skills would deteriorate, or he might get injured. Nevertheless, the San Antonio Spurs decided to make David the number one pick in the 1987 NBA Draft. They could only hope that he was an investment whose value would increase over time.

And that is precisely what has happened. David stayed in shape by playing on the U.S. Olympic team in 1988. Two years later, after averaging 24.3 points and 12 rebounds in his first season, he was named NBA Rookie of the Year. Since then, the honors have continued to pile up. David played in the NBA All-Star Game in each of his first seven seasons. He was Defensive Player of the Year in 1992 and Most Valuable Player in 1995.

David is one of three great centers on the Dream Team. The others are Shaquille O'Neal of the Orlando Magic and Hakeem Olajuwon of the Houston Rockets. No one is quite sure how the three players will be utilized, but David is excited about playing with Shaq and Hakeem.

"It's going to be unbelievable, I think," he says. "All three of us could be on the floor at the same time. It would be a pretty scary prospect for the other team. There's a lot of defense there, a lot of offense, a lot of quickness, everything."

David is also looking forward to matching up *against* Shaq and Hakeem in practice sessions. "When you put the USA jersey on and you see the quality of the guys who set foot on that floor every day, that makes you rise," he says. "The energy level is pumping, and you know there's never a time when you will have the same experiences."

Just the facts...
About David Robinson

Career Statistics

GP	FG%	FT%	Rebounds	Assists	Points	Avg.
475	.527	.744	5,921	1,471	12,209	25.7

Career Highlights

- Number one pick in 1987 NBA Draft
- Member of U.S. Olympic team in 1988, 1992, and 1996
- Named NBA Most Valuable Player in 1995
- Seven-time NBA All-Star

Did you know?

David Robinson was an outstanding high school student. By the time he was 14 years old he was taking advanced courses in computer technology at a local college.

GLENN ROBINSON

"We're not going to try to be like the first Dream Team. We're just going to be ourselves. We're going to do the best we can."

When Glenn Robinson was an All-American forward at Purdue University, they called him "Big Dog." He was so much quicker and stronger than everyone else that he was virtually unstoppable. It seemed that NBA stardom was his destiny.

Still, even Glenn, a 6' 7", 220-pound forward for the Milwaukee Bucks, didn't expect to be quite *this* big. In the summer of 1995, shortly after completing his rookie season, he became the youngest player selected to the United States Olympic men's basketball team that will compete this summer in Atlanta, Georgia. At only 22 years of age, Glenn was a member of the Dream Team.

"I was very surprised," he says. "Not only because I was a rookie, but because I'd be getting a chance to play with so many big-name players. Most of the guys I've been watching since I was in junior high. That's very exciting."

Anyone who's followed Glenn Robinson's career knows something about excitement. Since his high school days in Gary, Indiana, he has been a spectacular offensive player — a scoring machine who can shoot and handle the ball like a guard, and post up like a center. "He's very talented," says San Antonio Spurs center David Robinson. "He's an exciting type of player because he can do it all. He can rebound, he can score, he can run with you."

While Glenn is unquestionably among the most promising and

entertaining young players in the NBA, he is anything but flashy off the court. Unlike many professional athletes, he's not particularly interested in commercial endorsements or branching out into other fields. Glenn simply wants to play ball.

"His main focus really is on playing basketball," says Bucks coach Mike Dunleavy. "I don't think he has a lot of ulterior motives to have the game turn him into a politician or a TV commentator. He's content just being who he is."

Mr. Basketball

At Roosevelt High School in Gary, Glenn was a first-class athlete and citizen. In 1991, as a senior, he averaged 25.6 points, 14.6 rebounds, and 3.8 blocks, leading Roosevelt to a 30–1 record and a state championship. When the season was over Glenn was named Indiana's "Mr. Basketball." He also shared National Player of the Year honors with future NBA star Chris Webber, who played high school ball in Detroit. By the time he left Roosevelt, Glenn was the school's all-time leading scorer with 1,710 points.

Unfortunately, while Glenn was a good kid who had developed into one of the finest prep basketball players in the country, he was not one of the best students. He accepted a full athletic scholarship to Purdue University in West Lafayette, Indiana, but had to sit out his freshman year and concentrate on his classwork. As a sophomore, though, he was nothing less than sensational. Glenn averaged 24.1 points and 9.2 rebounds. He was named Purdue's Most Valuable Player and National Newcomer of the Year by *Basketball Times* magazine. Obviously, his skills had not diminished during his year off.

As impressive as Glenn's sophomore season was, though, it was nothing compared to his junior year. He led the nation in scoring with a 30.3 average. No Big Ten Athletic Conference player had achieved that feat since 1966! But he was more than just a scorer. Glenn became the first player in Purdue history to accumulate more than 1,000 points, 500 rebounds, 100 assists, 100 steals, and 50 blocks.

Glenn decided to leave college and play professional basketball after his junior year. Every team in the NBA wanted him on its roster, but the Milwaukee Bucks, as winners of the Draft Lottery, had the number one pick. To no one's surprise, they chose Glenn.

The Big Dog did not have much of a bite early in his first season. It took him a while to get in shape, and to adjust to the rigors of NBA competition. Like most rookies, Glenn discovered that he could never relax the way he had in college. He had to play as hard as he could — in practice and in games. After a while, Glenn began to play the way he was capable of playing. Teammates and opponents alike were impressed by his talent, as well as his hustle and desire.

One player Glenn really admired when he was growing up was Chicago Bulls forward Scottie Pippen. After getting a close look at his Dream Team teammate, Pippen had become a fan of Glenn's, as well. "He's a very, very talented player," Pippen says.

Glenn finished his first season as the Bucks' leading scorer (21.9) and second-leading rebounder (6.4). He was named to the NBA All-Rookie First Team. Those honors, of course, were nice, but nothing made Glenn happier than the phone call he received in June, when he was offered a chance to represent the United States in Olympic competition.

"I feel very proud," Glenn says. "It's only my second year in the pros and I've already had a chance to play in the Olympic Games. It's probably the best thing that's happened to me so far."

It's not a bad thing to have happened to the United States, either. The 1996 U.S. Olympic Dream Team is loaded with talent at every position, but there is room for a player as unselfish and talented as Glenn. Just ask Detroit Pistons forward Grant Hill, who is also a member of the 1996 U.S. Olympic Team. Grant came into the league in 1994, with Glenn, and so far he likes what he's seen. "Offensively, Big Dog can do it all," Hill says. "If I'm on the court with him, I'll get him the ball and let him do his thing. He's definitely the man."

Just the facts...
About Glenn Robinson

Career Statistics

GP	FG%	FT%	Rebounds	Assists	Points	Avg.
80	.451	.796	513	197	1,755	21.9

Career Highlights

- College Player of the Year in 1994
- NCAA scoring champion in 1993–94
- Number one pick in 1994 NBA Draft
- Led Milwaukee Bucks in scoring as a rookie (1994–95)

Did you know?

Glenn Robinson is only the third number one draft pick in Milwaukee Bucks history. The others were Kareem Abdul-Jabbar (formerly known as Lew Alcindor;1969) and Kent Benson (1977).

JOHN STOCKTON

"Because of the nature of the Dream Team, there's plenty of support whether we are home or abroad. But being home, having literally everybody there on our side, will be even more special. The expectations will be so high."

ohn Stockton has been around the game of basketball for a long time. At 34 years of age, with 12 years of NBA experience under his belt, he is the oldest member of the 1996 U.S. Olympic Dream Team. He is also one of the most decorated. John, a 6' 1" point guard with the Utah Jazz, has led the NBA in assists for eight consecutive seasons. In 1995 he eclipsed the great Magic Johnson as the NBA's career leader in that category.

For the longest time people wondered whether John was strong enough to play in the NBA. After all, he weighs only 175 pounds, which makes him one of the smallest players in the league. But they've long since stopped asking that question. No one runs a fast break like John Stockton. No one sees the court as well. No one plays harder.

"I think he's the best point guard ever, without a doubt," says Utah Jazz coach Jerry Sloan. "Because of his size and the fact that we haven't had a great center in his career, the things he has accomplished are nothing short of sensational."

John has nothing left to prove, but there are a few things he'd like to accomplish. Like winning an NBA championship and another gold medal. John played on the original U.S. Olympic Dream Team, which breezed through the 1992 Olympic Games in Barcelona, Spain. But that experience was both rewarding and frustrating. John suffered a slight fracture in his right leg during pre-Olympic workouts in Portland, Oregon, and was little more than a spectator during the games. He played in just four games and had a total of eight assists, far fewer than he typically records on a single night.

So, while John was proud to represent his country in 1992, and happy to accept the gold medal, he is even more excited about playing in the 1996 Olympic Games in Atlanta.

"It's the opportunity of a lifetime, even if you've already done it," John says. "Hopefully, we'll go in at full strength. Last time was disappointing mostly from the standpoint that I couldn't really practice after Portland. Those scrimmages were something to watch and I'm sure they were something to play in. And I didn't get that opportunity. I guess I'm looking forward to that the most in this new opportunity."

One thing is for certain: When John takes the floor in Atlanta, the folks back home in Spokane, Washington, will be watching. It's a ritual on winter nights. Friends gather at Jack and Dan's, a local restaurant owned by John's father, Jack Stockton. Thanks to a satellite hookup, friends and family watch all of the Jazz games. They sit together and applaud as the local boy slices through defenses and dishes out one gorgeous pass after another.

John was a very good high school player at Gonzaga Prep in Spokane. His size, though, prevented many colleges from recruiting him. He decided to attend Gonzaga University, located just a few blocks from his home. While there, John went from a scrawny 148 pounds to a well-muscled 175. He developed a pretty good jump shot. In four years he averaged 12.5 points and 5.2 assists. And in his senior year he averaged 20.9 points and 7.2 assists.

Those numbers convinced several NBA teams to look closely at John before the NBA draft. The average fan had no idea who he was, but NBA scouts were well aware of what he could do. John had an uncanny ability to see what was happening on the floor. Sometimes it seemed as though he had eyes in the back of his head. He never missed an open man on the break, and he rarely turned the ball over.

He also worked as hard as any player in college basketball. John was tireless and far more durable than he appeared. Small and baby-faced, he looked like a high school kid who had stumbled into the wrong gym — until he started playing. Once he started moving, John made it clear that intelligence and unselfishness were only part of his arsenal. He had tremendous athletic ability, as well. After interviewing John and his coaches, and watching him work out, the Jazz decided to take a chance on him. They made him the sixteenth pick in the 1984 draft. As it turned out, John wasn't much of a risk. He has become one of the most productive point guards in NBA history. Going into the 1995-96 season he has averaged 13.4 points and 11.6 assists per game. He is an eight-time NBA All-Star. And in 1994 and 1995 he was named to the All-NBA First Team.

A Tough Competitor

Along the way, John has earned the admiration of fans and teammates, and the respect of opponents. He is a fiesty tough competitor who never backs down from a challenge. That attitude was instilled in him when he was a youngster, playing one-on-one with his brother in backyard games. Behind the basket was a brick wall. Along one sideline was a picket fence. More than once, John lost a little skin diving for loose balls.

"He may look like an altar boy," says John's father. "But there's a lot of street in that kid."

The sight of John on a fast break, confidently pushing the ball up the floor and then flipping a no-look pass to Karl Malone has become one of the most common NBA highlights. But it's still a beautiful play — as long as you're a Jazz fan. If you happen to be the unfortunate defender assigned to stop John, you're in for a long night.

There are other reasons to admire John. Although he is a fierce competitor, he is a clean player. Off the court, he is a quiet, dignified man who likes to spend time with his wife and kids. As he approaches the end of his career, John thinks about how fortunate he has been. He never even expected to make it to the NBA. But here he is, a perennial All-Star and two-time Dream Teamer. He knows this will be his last Olympic appearance, and he wants to make the most of it.

"Everybody's expectations are for the gold," John says. "I know mine are. I don't think anybody would settle for anything less."

Just the facts...
About John Stockton

Career Statistics

GP	FG%	FT%	Rebounds	Assists	Points	Avg.
898	.515	.820	2,379	10,394	12,076	13.4

Career Highlights

- Named All-NBA First Team in 1994 and 1995
- Eight-time NBA All-Star
- All-time NBA leader in assists
- Won Olympic gold medal in 1992

Did you know?

Heading into the 1995-1996 season, John Stockton was number two in steals on the NBA's all-time list, trailing only Maurice Cheeks.

Jennifer Azzi goes up strong.

USA Basketball Women's National Team

On May 24, 1995, USA Basketball selected 11 of the finest athletes in the country to form the USA Basketball Women's National Team. These women, all of whom were collegiate stars, will be the nucleus of the 1996 United States Olympic women's basketball team. Like their male counterparts, they have been brought together with one goal in mind: to win a gold medal in Atlanta.

For this "Dream Team," though, the task is a bit more difficult. Women's basketball became an Olympic medal sport in 1976. Americans won the gold medal for the first time in 1984, and then repeated in 1988. But the United States has enjoyed only modest international success in women's basketball in recent years.

The formation of the USA Basketball Women's National Team represents a serious attempt to reverse that trend. In the past, the teams were assembled a couple of months before the Olympic Games. The coaches and players introduced themselves, tried to get a feel for their abilities, and did the best they could. Sometimes it was enough. Sometimes it wasn't.

This time the approach is completely different. For the past ten months these women have been living together, traveling together, training together, and playing together. They have made tremendous personal and professional sacrifices because they are thoroughly dedicated to this cause.

"It became apparent that the United States could no longer select its players, train for a short period of time, and expect to win a gold medal," says Carol Callan, USA Basketball Women's National Team director. "The USA Basketball Women's National Team is an exciting step, and one we feel will help lift the USA back on top."

Considering the popularity of basketball in this country, it might seem strange that the United States has struggled in most major competitions over the last five years. But there is a simple explanation. While the number of girls playing high school basketball has increased and the quality of the women's game at the collegiate level has improved dramatically, there are few opportunities for women after they graduate from college. The best male players move on to the NBA. But there are no professional leagues for women in the United States currently, so the best female players must seek employment in Europe or Japan.

Each of the members of the USA Basketball Women's National Team is receiving a $50,000 salary. By NBA standards, of course, that isn't much. But it's more than they've ever been offered to play in the United States before. Most important of all, the concept of a national team demonstrates to the players that USA Basketball is committed not only to winning a gold medal, but to the sport of women's basketball.

"I think this team is a great step for women's basketball," says Dawn Staley, a former All-America point guard from Virginia who hopes to be representing the United States in Atlanta. "Americans will see a much improved level of play when players return to the

USA from their professional teams. People may start to understand that women basketball players — all basketball players — play their best ball after college. Maybe this team could even lead to a spin-off to a women's professional league in the United States."

The U.S. Olympic women's basketball team will be coached by Tara VanDerveer and may include the following players. (The roster could change following the publication of this book.)

Jennifer Azzi:

Naismith Player of the year as a senior at Stanford in 1990, when the Cardinal won the NCAA championship; played professionally in Sweden in 1994–95 and averaged 31.6 points per game.

Ruthie Bolton:

An excellent outside shooter who hit 52.6 percent of her three-point attempts in the 1994 Goodwill Games.

Lisa Leslie takes it to the hole.

Teresa Edwards:

Could become the first American basketball player — male or female — to compete in four Olympiads. Second-leading scorer on the 1988 U.S. Olympic team, which won a gold medal in Seoul, South Korea.

Lisa Leslie:

A strong inside player who led the University of Southern California in scoring and rebounding as a junior and senior; National High School Player of the Year in 1990. Earned All-Pacific-10 Conference first team honors in all four of her seasons.

Rebecca Lobo:

The youngest member of the team; a versatile center who led Connecticut to a 35–0 record and the NCAA title in 1995; named 1995 College Player of the Year.

Katrina McClain:

A veteran forward who has played professionally in Europe and Asia for the past seven years; named USA Basketball Female Athlete of the Year in 1992; a member of the 1988 and 1992 U.S. Olympic teams.

Nikki McCray:

Former University of Tennessee guard who was voted the Southeastern Conference Player of the Year in 1994 and 1995. Led the Lady Vols during her four seasons to an overall record of 122-11

Carla McGhee:

A power forward who helped the University of Tennessee win two national titles in 1987 and 1989; has played professionally in Germany, Italy, Switzerland, and Spain.

Dawn Staley:

Holds NCAA career record for steals with 454; a quick guard who led the University of Virginia to three consecutive NCAA Final Four appearances. Voted College player of the Year in 1991 and 1992.

Katy Steding:

A good long-range shooter. Played on Stanford's national championship team in 1990, and set an NCAA record by hitting six three-pointers in a Final Four game.

Sheryl Swoopes:

Named 1993 National Player of the Year by *USA Today* and *Sports Illustrated*, among others. Scored 47 points in Texas Tech's 84–82 victory over Ohio State in the '93 NCAA championship game.

There is no question that the United States has an exceptionally talented team, one that is quite capable of winning an Olympic gold medal. It's also a team that could give women's basketball the exposure it so richly deserves. For many of the players, that would be a tremendous accomplishment — almost like winning another medal.

USA Basketball Women's National Team Roster

No.	Name	Pos.	Ht.	Wt.	Birth Date	College
8	Jennifer Azzi	Guard	5'8"	140	8/31/68	Stanford
6	Ruthie Bolton	Guard	5'8"	150	5/25/67	Auburn
4	Teresa Edwards	Guard	5'11"	155	7/19/64	Georgia
9	Lisa Leslie	Fwd/Ctr	6'5"	170	7/7/72	USC
13	Rebecca Lobo	Fwd/Ctr	6'4"	190	10/6/73	Connecticut
12	Katrina McClain	Forward	6'2"	180	9/19/65	Georgia
15	Nikki McCray	Guard	5'11"	158	12/17/71	Tennessee
10	Carla McGhee	Fwd/Ctr	6'2"	170	3/6/68	Tennessee
5	Dawn Staley	Guard	5'6"	128	5/4/70	Virginia
11	Katy Steding	Forward	6'0"	160	12/11/67	Stanford
7	Sheryl Swoopes	Guard	6'0"	145	3/25/71	Texas Tech

Coach: Tara VanDerveer, Stanford University

The Coach

Even though Tara VanDerveer was excited about representing the United States in the Olympic Games, she did not immediately agree to become head coach of the USA Basketball Women's National Team that was selected in the spring of 1995. Coaching the national team, which would form the nucleus of the U.S. Olympic team in 1996, involved a year-long commitment. That meant VanDerveer would have to take a leave of absence from her job as coach of Stanford University's women's basketball team.

She wrestled with the decision for several months. VanDerveer had built an extremely successful program at Stanford, and she felt guilty about leaving her players. But in the end, the lure of Olympic gold was too tempting to ignore. It was, VanDerveer realized, the opportunity of a lifetime.

VanDerveer's credentials are outstanding. She is one of the most accomplished coaches in the college game. In 10 years at Stanford she has won two national championships and compiled a career record of 251–62. Coaching an Olympic team, of course, presents an entirely different challenge. But Vanderveer, who has a wealth of international experience, seems ideally suited to the task.

"I'm extremely focused on doing the very best job I can for this team," VanDerveer says. "When you're representing your country, it's not something you want to mess up."

The original Deam Team — perhaps the greatest
basketball team ever assembled.

The Original Dream Team

When USA Basketball assembled the first Dream Team, it did so with one very specific goal in mind: to win a gold medal at the 1992 Olympic Games in Barcelona, Spain. Anything less would be unacceptable. In fact, anything less would be an embarrassment.

In the past, Olympic basketball competition had been closed to NBA players, which meant that the United States had been represented primarily by college players. Now, though, the rules were different. We were sending our best players — the *world's* best players. For the first time, NBA superstars such as Michael Jordan, Larry Bird, and Magic Johnson would wear the U.S. Olympic uniform. They were excited about the opportunity, of course, but they also felt quite a bit of pressure. Not only were they expected to win the gold medal, they were expected to dominate the tournament.

"There's no question in my mind that I'll be coaching what may be the greatest array of stars ever assembled," coach Chuck Daly said before the start of the Olympic Games. "But that doesn't necessarily mean the greatest team. That will be the primary challenge facing the coaching staff: To try, in a very short period of time, to bring this group together as a team."

Chuck Daly is the kind of coach who worries a lot, and the

stress and excitement of representing his country caused him to lose sleep in the weeks leading up to the Olympic Games. In the end, though, there was little reason for concern. There was no jealousy on the Dream Team. Each of these professionals was a superstar on his NBA team, but each was quite willing to play a less prominent role if it meant the team would benefit.

Choosing the original Dream Team was a difficult task. But after much discussion and evaluation, a panel of USA Basketball officials extended invitations to the following players: Charles Barkley, forward, Philadelphia 76ers (traded to the Phoenix Suns prior to the Olympic Games); Larry Bird, forward, Boston Celtics; Clyde Drexler, guard, Portland Trail Blazers; Patrick Ewing, center, New York Knicks; Magic Johnson, guard, Los Angeles Lakers; Michael Jordan, guard, Chicago Bulls; Karl Malone, forward, Utah Jazz; Chris Mullin, forward, Golden State Warriors; Scottie Pippen, forward, Chicago Bulls; David Robinson, center, San Antonio Spurs; John Stockton, guard, Utah Jazz. Christian Laettner, a center who had just finished his senior year at Duke University, was the only college player invited.

The Dream Team worked toward its goal with a sense of urgency. Each day in practice these 12 stars tore into each other like kids on a playground. They weren't concerned about getting hurt or seeing their names in headlines. They simply tried as hard as they could to get ready for the Olympic Games. "The practices were incredible," recalls David Robinson. "I've never seen so many talented guys go at each other so hard before. The practices were the best part of the whole experience."

The games were predictably one-sided. From the opening tip of the opening contest, it was no contest. Not once did the Dream

Team get caught napping. They won eight games by an average of 44 points and easily won the gold medal. "The camaraderie was great," says Scottie Pippen. "When you're playing with the greatest talent in the world, you feel like you're unbeatable. And we were."

1992 U.S. Olympic Dream Team Stats

Name	Points/Avg.	REB/Avg.	Assists
Charles Barkley	144/18.0	33/4.1	19
Larry Bird	67/8.4	30/3.8	14
Clyde Drexler	84/10.5	24/3.0	29
Patrick Ewing	76/9.5	42/5.3	3
Magic Johnson	48/8.0	14/2.3	33
Michael Jordan	119/14.9	19/2.4	38
Christian Laettner	38/4.8	20/2.5	3
Karl Malone	104/13.0	42/5.3	9
Chris Mullin	103/12.9	13/1.6	29
Scottie Pippen	72/9.0	17/2.1	47
David Robinson	72/9.0	33/4.1	7
John Stockton	11/2.8	1/0.3	8

Team Results

USA 116, Angola 48

USA 103, Croatia 70

USA 111, Germany 68

USA 127, Brazil 83

USA 122, Spain 81

USA 115, Puerto Rico 77

USA 127, Lithuania 76

USA 117, Croatia 85

The 1994
Dream Team

The team that represented the United States at the 1994 World
Championship in Toronto, Canada, had a tough act to fol-
low. The original Dream Team had secured a place in history by
easily winning a gold medal at the Olympic Games in Barcelona,
Spain. With that performance the United States formally introduced the grace and power of the NBA to a worldwide audience.

Now, another version of the Dream Team was expected to shred

the opposition in similar fashion. The expectations, however, were a bit unrealistic. After all, the first Dream Team had included a handful of the greatest players in the history of the game. It was a team comprised largely of veterans hungry for one shot at Olympic gold. They were playing under unique circumstances. The 1994 Dream Team, coached by Don Nelson, was a much younger squad. How could they compete with the legend of the original Dream Team?

Not that there wasn't talent on this Dream Team. There was plenty of it. The final roster included the following players: Derrick Coleman, forward, New Jersey Nets; Joe Dumars, guard, Detroit Pistons; Shawn Kemp, forward, Seattle SuperSonics; Kevin Johnson, guard, Phoenix Suns; Larry Johnson, forward, Charlotte Hornets; Dan Majerle, guard, Phoenix Suns; Reggie Miller, guard, Indiana Pacers; Alonzo Mourning, center, Charlotte Hornets; Shaquille O'Neal, center, Orlando Magic; Mark Price, guard, Cleveland Cavaliers; Steve Smith, guard, Miami Heat; Dominique Wilkins, forward, Los Angeles Clippers/Boston Celtics.

Any team that features Shaq in the middle and Reggie Miller at shooting guard has to be considered a formidable outfit, and the Dream Team was no exception. Like their predecessors on the original Dream Team, the players were eager to bring home a gold medal. "I had a great time in Toronto," Miller remembers. "I was like a kid in a candy store. I was excited just to be on the team. But then to be named one of the tri-captains and have a chance to start—I was in heaven."

The Dream Team did as expected and won the world title. But its road to the gold medal was not nearly as smooth as the one taken by the first Dream Team. In its opening game, for example, the United States trailed Spain by one point late in the first half. Nothing like that had happened to the original Dream Team, whose games were usually decided in the first few minutes. Comparisons between the two Dream Teams had been drawn, of course, and now it looked like the sequel was going to be a pale imitation of the original.

In the second half, however, the United States was a different team. The jitters were gone, and the fluid graceful style of play so commonly seen in the NBA was back on display. The Dream Team went on a 16–0 run early in the second half and escaped with a 115–100 victory. "I'm glad we won, but I'm very disappointed," Miller said afterward. "We've got to play with more intensity. This was a good wake-up call."

The 1994 Dream Team had learned what the 1992 Dream Team knew instinctively: Even the best players in the world can't take anything for granted. That lesson carried over into the next night's game, an impressive 132–77 rout of China. "We played harder and we played together," said Shaquille O'Neal, who had 22 points in just 18 minutes. "I think we took a step in the right direction."

Apparently so. The United States was tested only once the rest of the way, in a 111–94 quarterfinal victory over Russia. The Dream Team defeated Greece by 39 points in the semifinals, and then hammered Russia 137–91 in the championship game. Shaq, who had just finished his second year in the NBA, emerged from the World Championship as basketball's newest star. He led the Dream Team in both scoring (18.0) and rebounding (8.5). With his impressive combination of strength and agility, he left both teammates and opponents in awe.

"There isn't anything he can't do," Kevin Johnson said. "I used to be one of those people who never really believed all the hype surrounding him. But after playing alongside him for a couple of weeks, I believe now."

1994 Dream Team Stats

Name	Points/Avg.	REB/Avg.	Assists
Derrick Coleman	69/8.6	31/3.9	6
Joe Dumars	88/12.6	10/1.4	20
Shawn Kemp	75/9.4	54/6.8	12
Kevin Johnson	40/5.0	14/1.8	31
Larry Johnson	49/6.1	41/5.1	7
Dan Majerle	70/8.8	18/2.3	13
Reggie Miller	137/17.1	13/1.6	18
Alonzo Mourning	87/10.9	41/5.1	5
Shaquille O'Neal	144/18.0	68/8.5	4
Mark Price	77/9.6	20/2.5	29
Steve Smith	24/3.0	10/1.3	14
Dominique Wilkins	101/12.6	26/3.3	8

Team Results

USA 115, Spain 100	USA 134, Puerto Rico 83
USA 132, China 77	USA 111, Russia 94
USA 105, Brazil 82	USA 97, Greece 58
USA 130, Australia 74	USA 137, Russia 91

Dream Team Quiz

1) Which Dream Team player attended the U.S. Naval Academy?

   A) Grant Hill

   B) David Robinson

   C) Reggie Miller

2) What is Karl Malone's nickname?

   A) Big Dog

   B) The Enforcer

   C) The Mailman

3) Who is the heaviest member of the Dream Team?

   A) David Robinson

   B) Shaquille O'Neal

   C) Hakeem Olajuwon

4) Who is the lightest member of the Dream Team?

   A) John Stockton

   B) Anfernee Hardaway

   C) Glenn Robinson

5) Who is the oldest member of the Dream Team?

   A) Hakeem Olajuwon

   B) Karl Malone

   C) John Stockton

6) Choose the player whose father was a star running back in the National Football League.

   A) Glenn Robinson
   B) Scottie Pippen
   C) Grant Hill

7) Who coached the Dream Team at the 1994 World Championship?

   A) Don Nelson
   B) Don Chaney
   C) Mike Krzyzewski

8) Choose the player who has been a member of three U.S. Olympic Teams.

   A) Hakeem Olajuwon
   B) David Robinson
   C) John Stockton

9) What is the average weight of the Dream Team?

   A) 245 pounds
   B) 220 pounds
   C) 230 pounds

10) What is the average height of the Dream Team?

    A) 6'8"
    B) 6'6"
    C) 6'10"

11) What is the average age of the Dream Team?

   A) 26
   B) 30
   C) 28

12) What is the average shoe size of the Dream Team?

   A) 11
   B) 13
   C) 15

13) The Dream Team has how many combined years of NBA experience?

   A) 71
   B) 48
   C) 121

14) In international competition, how far from the basket is the three-point line?

   A) 22 feet
   B) 20 feet, 6.1 inches
   C) 21 feet, 6 inches

15) In international competition, each team has how much time to attempt a shot?

   A) 30 seconds
   B) 45 seconds
   C) 24 seconds

16) The United States has lost only two games in Olympic history. To which country did the United States lose both games?

A) Japan
B) Soviet Union
C) Spain

17) Which member of the original Dream Team did not win a gold medal at the 1984 Olympic Games?

A) Michael Jordan
B) Patrick Ewing
C) John Stockton

18) The Dream Team won the gold medal at the World Championship in 1994. In what city was the tournament held?

A) Madrid, Spain
B) Milan, Italy
C) Toronto, Canada

19) Who is the youngest member of the Dream Team?

A) Glenn Robinson
B) Grant Hill
C) Anfernee Hardaway

20) Which member of the Dream Team played the most minutes at the 1994 World Championship?

A) Derrick Coleman
B) Reggie Miller
C) Joe Dumars

21) Which player did not start for the Dream Team in the first game of the 1992 Olympic Games?

A) Larry Bird
B) Michael Jordan
C) Magic Johnson

22) Which member of the original Dream Team has won a state high school championship, an NCAA title, an Olympic gold medal, and an NBA championship?

A) Larry Bird
B) Patrick Ewing
C) Magic Johnson

23) Dream Team coach Lenny Wilkens is the head coach of which NBA team?

A) Boston Celtics
B) Sacramento Kings
C) Atlanta Hawks

24) In what city was Shaquille O'Neal born?

A) Newark, New Jersey
B) Los Angeles, California
C) Orlando, Florida

25) Which country did the Dream Team defeat to win the gold medal at the 1992 Olympic Games in Barcelona?

A) Croatia
B) Italy
C) Canada

26) Which player led the original Dream Team in scoring?

A) Scottie Pippen
B) Charles Barkley
C) Michael Jordan

27) Who is the only player to make a Dream Team roster without having played an NBA game?

A) Christian Laettner
B) Anfernee Hardaway
C) Kevin Johnson

28) Clyde Drexler of the original Dream Team and Hakeem Olajuwon of the 1996 Dream Team were college teammates. Can you name their school?

A) UCLA
B) University of Kentucky
C) University of Houston

29) Which team did the United States defeat to win the gold medal at the 1994 World Championship?

A) Russia
B) China
C) Angola

ANSWERS: 1-B, 2-C, 3-B, 4-A, 5-C, 6-C, 7-A, 8-B, 9-C, 10-A, 11-C, 12-C, 13-A, 14-B, 15-A, 16-B, 17-C, 18-C, 19-A, 20-B, 21-A, 22-C, 23-C, 24-A, 25-A, 26-B, 27-A, 28-C, 29-A

About the Author

Joe Layden is the former award-winning sports editor and columnist for the Albany (New York) *Times Union*. He is the author of several books for children. Mr. Layden lives in Saratoga Springs, New York, with his wife Susan and his daughter, Emily.